JONAH

A PROPHET ON THE RUN

Other studies in the Not Your Average Bible Study series

Ruth

Psalms

Malachi

Sermon on the Mount

Ephesians

Colossians

Hebrews

James

1 Peter

2 Peter and Jude

1–3 John

For updates on this series, visit lexhampress.com/nyab

JONAH

A PROPHET
ON THE RUN

NOT YOUR AVERAGE BIBLE STUDY

MILES CUSTIS

B^s **Bible Study**
MAGAZINE

LEXHAM PRESS

Jonah: A Prophet on the Run
Not Your Average Bible Study

Adapted with permission from content originally published in *Bible Study Magazine* (Issues 6.2–6.3)

Lexham Press, 1313 Commercial St., Bellingham, WA 98225
LexhamPress.com

ISBN: 978-1-57-799554-8

Editor-in-Chief: John D. Barry
Managing Editor: Rebecca Van Noord
Assistant Editors: Elizabeth Vince, Joel Wilcox, Jessi Strong
Cover Design: Christine Gerhart
Typesetting: projectluz.com

CONTENTS

HOW TO USE
THIS RESOURCE

Not Your Average Bible Study is a series of in-depth Bible studies that can be used for individual or group study. Depending on your individual needs or your group pace, you may opt to cover one lesson a week or more.

Each lesson prompts you to dig deep into the Word—as such, we recommend you use your preferred translation with this study. The author used his own translation, but included quotations from the English Standard Version. Whatever Bible version you use, please be sure you leave ample time to get into the Bible itself.

To assist you, we recommend using the Faithlife Study Bible, which contains notes written by Miles Custis and is also edited by John D. Barry. You can download this digital resource for free for your tablet, phone, personal computer, or use it online. Go to FaithlifeBible.com to learn more.

May God bless you in the study of His Word.

INTRODUCTION

The biblical prophets often serve as models of obedience and righteousness, but Jonah's story is one of rebellion and self-centeredness. When God calls Jonah to preach to the Ninevites, he flees in the opposite direction. And when the Ninevites repent and receive God's mercy, Jonah sulks instead of celebrating. Yet Jonah's story provides us with a portrait of God's mercy and determination to bring all people back to Himself. Even though Jonah saw the Ninevites as his enemy, God saw a people who desperately needed Him. Jonah's story compels us to pray that our enemies will come to know God's saving grace through Jesus Christ—and that our priorities are so aligned with God's that we will celebrate when they do.

JONAH 1–2

As children, we learned of Jonah being swallowed by a "big fish" and then spewed out after three days. This seemingly climactic moment is just one of several obstacles Jonah faced while evading God's commands (see Jonah 1:4; 4:6–8). However, by focusing so much on Jonah and the fish, we (like Jonah) might downplay the greatest miracle of all: the entire city of Nineveh repenting and turning to God (3:4–10).

Miraculous events are often only a means of communicating a more important message. As we read Jonah, let's focus on the message behind the marvels: God's concern for all people and the miracle of His salvation.

READING JONAH

 Pray that God will give you wisdom as you study the book of Jonah.

Read the entire book of Jonah aloud in one sitting.

The story of Jonah being swallowed by a "great fish" is familiar enough that we might be tempted to skim the text. As you read the book of Jonah, imagine you are encountering it for the first time. At different junctures, pause and ask yourself what you expect to happen next. How does the story defy your expectations? What details had you not noticed before? How do they add to your understanding of the book?

_____

_____

_____

_____

When we read narrative, it is important that we pay attention to character portrayal. Does Jonah measure up to the expectations you have for a prophet? Are Jonah's responses to God's instructions and actions fitting for his role?

_____

_____

_____

How does Jonah interact with God? Consider the sailors and the people of Nineveh. How do their responses to God differ from Jonah's?

_____

_____

_____

A PROPHET ON THE RUN

 Pray that you would be open and responsive to God's call in your life.

Read Jonah 1:1–6. Reflect on Jonah 1:1–3.

The book of Jonah begins like many of the prophetic books: God's word is announced to His messenger (compare Joel 1:1; Mic 1:1; Jer 1:4). In Jonah's case, God's instructions consist of only one verse describing the wickedness of a distant city in a foreign land. What does this tell us about the nature of God's concern (compare Psa 24:1; Prov 15:3)?

_____

_____

_____

Read Psalm 94:8–11 and Jeremiah 23:23–24. What do these passages say about God's ability to see the hearts of all people?

_____

_____

_____

Instead of heading toward Nineveh (to the east of Israel), Jonah boards a ship heading to Tarshish—the westernmost location in the ancient Near East. Notice that Jonah is described as going "away from the presence of the Lord" (a phrase that is repeated twice in Jonah 1:3). What do you think Jonah was trying to accomplish?

_____

_____

_____

Compare Genesis 3:8. Have you ever tried to hide or escape from God's presence? If so, why?

_____

_____

_____

Jonah's action contrasts with the prophets' typical responses to God's call. Read Isaiah 6:8 and Hosea 1:2–3. How did these prophets answer God's call? Think of a time you felt God's call to act. How did you respond?

_____

_____

_____

GOD IN PURSUIT

Pray that you would not despise the discipline of the Lord.

Read Jonah 1:1–10. Reflect on Jonah 1:4–6.

Jonah attempts to get "away from the presence of the LORD" in Jonah 1:3. We soon see that he cannot escape the LORD's presence (1:4). Read Psalm 139:1–12. How does this psalm describe God's knowledge of our actions and attitudes? Do you find that comforting or intimidating, and why?

_____

_____

_____

_____

God sends a mighty storm, and the ship threatens "to break up" (Jonah 1:4). Do you see the storm as God's punishment against Jonah or His way of getting the prophet back on the right track? How do you think Jonah understood it?

_____

_____

_____

_____

Read Hebrews 12:5–11. How have you responded to God's discipline?

_____

_____

_____

_____

Compare the sailors' reactions to the storm with Jonah's reaction. Why do you think Jonah was so calm while the sailors were so afraid?

_____

_____

_____

The sailors all called out to their gods, and the captain encouraged Jonah to do the same (see Jonah 1:6), but the text does not say whether he did. Perhaps Jonah didn't want God's help, or perhaps he was still attempting to flee from God's presence. Have you ever avoided asking God for help? Why is that? Consider your reasons for doing so, and bring them to God. How can you turn to Him in your time of need?

_____

_____

_____

A FOOL FOR A PROPHET

Pray that the Spirit would help you live out your beliefs.

Read Jonah 1:4–10. Reflect on Jonah 1:7–10.

Desperate to quell the storm, the sailors cast lots. This may seem strange to us, but casting lots was a common way to determine responsibility or God's will (see 1 Sam 14:38–42; see also Prov 16:33; Acts 1:26).

Jonah speaks for the first time in the book when he answers the sailors' questions. He identifies himself and his God: "I am a Hebrew, and I fear the LORD" (Jonah 1:9). In the Old Testament, fearing God was an expression of loyalty, reverence and obedience (compare Deut 5:29; Josh 24:14–15; Psa 25:12–13). Has Jonah shown any evidence of "fearing" God with his actions? How do your actions back up your beliefs? What can you do to ensure your life is consistent with your faith?

_____

_____

_____

_____

Jonah's description of God—"the God of heaven, who made the sea and the dry land" (Jonah 1:9)—makes his attempt to flee seem foolish. How could Jonah expect to escape God when He is everywhere? Think back to a situation where you acted in a way that now seems foolish—why did you act the way you did? How can you respond differently to similar situations you face today?

_____

_____

_____

_____

REVERENT SAILORS

Pray that God would make you an effective witness of Christ's salvation.

Read Jonah 1:4–17. Reflect on Jonah 1:11–16.

The sailors, frightened and incredulous at Jonah's words, ask him what they can do to quiet the storm. With his answer, Jonah acknowledges his guilt for the first time. He does not repent or petition God to stop the storm. Instead he tells the sailors to throw him overboard. Is he sacrificing his life for the lives of the sailors, or is he still stubbornly refusing to obey God's call to Nineveh?

_____

_____

_____

_____

The sailors, unlike Jonah, react honorably. Instead of throwing Jonah overboard, they labor through the storm. Notice their prayer in Jonah 1:14. What did they fear? Of all those on board, who showed a more proper fear of God (see 1:9)?

_____

_____

_____

_____

Despite his reluctance and disobedience, Jonah was still an effective witness to the sailors. His "prophecy" in 1:12 proved true, and his portrayal of God as the creator of the sea was validated when the storm stopped. After their encounter with Jonah, the sailors publicly worship the LORD by sacrificing and making vows.

Read 1 Corinthians 1:26–31. Why does God use the foolish and weak of the world? How can God use you, in your weakness, to reach people with the truth of Christ?

_____

_____

_____

A FISH WITH AN APPOINTMENT

 Pray that the Holy Spirit would help you understand "the sign of Jonah."

Read Jonah 1:7–2:10. Reflect on Jonah 1:17.

The "great fish" swallowing Jonah is the enduring image of the book. Surprisingly, only three verses mention the fish (see Jonah 1:17; 2:1, 10). Why do you think people focus so much on this aspect of the story?

_____

_____

_____

The miraculous nature of the events described in 1:17 often leads people to contemplate how Jonah could have survived three days inside a great fish. Perhaps a better question is "Why?" What purpose does the fish serve in the story?

_____

_____

_____

What was Jonah expecting when he was thrown overboard? How did God use the fish to undermine Jonah's expectations and accomplish His purpose?

_____

_____

_____

_____

In the Gospels, Jesus refers to Jonah 1:17 when the Pharisees ask Him for a sign. Read Matthew 12:38–42 and 16:1–4. What are some parallels between Jonah's time in the belly of the fish and Jesus' time between the cross and His resurrection?

_____

_____

_____

What is the "sign" of Jonah in Matthew 12:38–42? How would that fulfill the Pharisees' request for a sign?

_____

_____

_____

Compare Luke 11:29–32. What is the "sign" of Jonah in that passage?

_____

_____

_____

THE PROPHET FINALLY PRAYS

 Pray that God would lead you to look first to Him in times of trouble.

Read Jonah 1:11–2:10. Reflect on Jonah 2:1–6

The prophet Jonah reaches out to God for the first time in the book in Jonah 2:1. The captain of the ship implored him to call out to God in 1:6, but we're never told that he did. Until now he had been trying to flee from God's presence (see 1:3, 10). Ironically, the prophet who thought he could escape God's presence now cries out to Him from the most unlikely of places: the belly of a fish. Why do you think Jonah did not pray until now?

_____

_____

_____

_____

When you're in the midst of trouble, how quickly do you reach out to God? Jonah's prayer in 2:2–9 resembles a psalm of thanksgiving (compare 2:2 with Psa 18:6; 34:4), in which the psalmist thanks God for delivering him. Yet Jonah is still in the belly of the fish, where we would expect a psalm of lament or a prayer for deliverance. Why do you think Jonah prayed this way? What stands out to you about his prayer?

_____

_____

_____

_____

_____

In Jonah 2:4, Jonah prays, "I am driven away from your sight," but in the previous chapter, he was the one trying to get away from God's presence. God had been working to bring him back on course. Can you look back on a time when it felt like God had abandoned you? Reflect on that time. Did God abandon you or did you avoid Him?

_____

_____

_____

_____

A GOD OF GRACE

 Pray that God would give you an appreciation of His salvation and a willingness to share it with others.

 Read Jonah 2:1–10. Reflect on Jonah 2:7–10.

In Jonah 2:7, the prophet states that he "remembered the LORD" as he was close to death. What do you suppose he remembered about God?

_____

_____

_____

Compare 2:7 with Jonah's statement about God in 4:2. How does the prophet's consideration of God's grace and mercy differ when he is the recipient rather than the people of Nineveh?

_____

_____

_____

_____

Read Psalm 77:11–15 and 143:5–6. Why is it important to remember what God has done in the past? How have you been encouraged by remembering the ways He has provided for you?

_____

_____

_____

_____

Read Joshua 4:1–7. What was the purpose of the stones? Do you do anything specific to remind yourself of God's ongoing provision or His faithfulness?

_____

_____

_____

Jonah concludes his prayer by triumphantly proclaiming, "Salvation belongs to the Lord!" (Jonah 2:9). In what ways do you see God's salvation revealed in the book of Jonah? Compare Jonah's and the sailors' reactions to God's deliverance (see 1:16; 2:9). What does this say about the scope and availability of God's salvation?

_____

_____

_____

After God speaks to the fish in 2:10, it spews Jonah out onto dry land. How does the fish respond to God's word compared to Jonah in 1:1–3? How do you respond to God's word?

_____

_____

_____

CONCLUSION

Sometimes God accomplishes His purposes in unusual ways. Jonah fled from Nineveh and God's presence instead of carrying out His instructions to preach to the people of that city. But God pursued Jonah and revealed Himself as "the God of heaven, who made the sea and the dry land" to the sailors (1:9). Whether through a great fish, a mighty storm, or the testimony of imperfect and rebellious people, God finds ways to bring people to Himself. May we respond faithfully to the work He wants to do in us and through us.

JONAH 3–4

Jonah never wanted to deliver God's warning of imminent destruction to the people of Nineveh, the capital of Assyria. Well-known for their violence and terrible cruelty, the Assyrians were a direct threat to the Israelites. Jonah saw Nineveh as his enemy, so when the Ninevites repented and God relented from punishing them, he was furious.

Jonah is a counterexample of what it means to love our enemies. He didn't want his enemies to receive the same mercy and grace he had come to expect from God. Many of us can relate. It seems to go against our instincts to love people who have hurt or wronged us. Yet God's love isn't restrained by our human labels of "friend" or "enemy." He goes to great lengths to bring all His creation back to Himself, as demonstrated by His compassion toward the infamous city of Nineveh. In the next eight lessons, we'll see how the book of Jonah compels us to pray that even our worst enemies will come to know God's saving grace through Jesus Christ.

REREADING JONAH

Pray that God will give you wisdom as you study the book of Jonah.

Read the entire book of Jonah aloud in one sitting.

The book of Jonah tells one complete story. Reading it through in one sitting gives you a better understanding of the story as a whole. As you read, look for repeated words or phrases, like "provided" or "appointed" (מנה). What words stand out to you? Note, for example, how frequently the word "great" appears. Although it may not always be translated as "great" in English Bibles, the Hebrew word for "great" (גדול, *gadol*) appears 15 times in the book. What does "great" describe in Jonah? What makes Jonah a "great" story?

_____

_____

_____

Think about the variety of God's attributes. Which are most prevalent in the book of Jonah?

_____

_____

_____

How does Jonah describe God in 1:9 and 4:2? Describe how these characteristics are demonstrated in the narrative. How have you seen them in your life?

_____

_____

_____

A SECOND CHANCE FOR OBEDIENCE

 Pray that the Holy Spirit would give you a sincere heart of faith and obedience.

Read Jonah 2:1–3:3. Reflect on Jonah 3:1–3.

At the beginning of chapter 3, God gives Jonah a second chance to obey, repeating His command for Jonah to go to Nineveh. Compare His call in 1:1–3 with that in 3:1–3. In 1:2 God speaks of the Ninevites' wickedness, but in 3:2 He emphasizes His role as the source of Jonah's message. Why do you think God changed the focus of His command?

_____

_____

_____

God willingly gives Jonah a second chance. What does this confirm about Jonah's descriptions of His character (compare 4:2)? Read 1 Timothy 1:16. How has God displayed His "perfect patience" in your life?

_____

_____

_____

Describe a time when God gave you a second chance. How can you display His patience to others (compare Matt 18:21–22)?

_____

_____

_____

Compare Jonah's different responses to God's commands. Do you think he had a change of heart since 1:3, or did he merely realize he could not escape from God's wishes? In light of Jonah's later prayer to God (see 4:1–4), which is more likely?

_____

_____

_____

Chances are we have all obeyed God begrudgingly or reluctantly at some point. Why is it important for us to be sincere in our faith (compare 1 Tim 1:5–7)?

_____

_____

_____

OVERWHELMING REPENTANCE

Pray that God would give you words to speak His message to others.

Read Jonah 3:1–5. Reflect on Jonah 3:4–5.

Finally, Jonah fulfills his call from the beginning of the book: He brings God's message to Nineveh. The message is short and negative: "In 40 days Nineveh will be destroyed." Compare Jonah's message to Nineveh with other prophecies against foreign nations, such as Jeremiah's prophecy against Babylon (Jer 51:1–58), Obadiah's prophecy against Edom (Obad 1–21), and Nahum's prophecy against Nineveh (Nah 3:1–19).

Despite Jonah's underwhelming message, the people of Nineveh responded immediately. The text emphasizes that they repented not because they believed Jonah, but because they "believed God" (Jonah 3:5). To what do you attribute their belief?

_____

_____

_____

_____

What does the Ninevites' enthusiastic response—despite Jonah's lack of enthusiasm—show you about God's ability to bring people to Himself? How does it encourage you to proclaim God's word to others?

_____

_____

_____

_____

In addition to believing God, the people of Nineveh also repented by fasting and wearing sackcloth—traditional activities of mourning. How would you describe the relationship between repentance and belief (compare Mark 1:15 and Acts 20:21)?

_____

_____

_____

Can you have true belief without repentance (see Acts 2:37–38)? What about repentance without belief (compare Exod 10:16–20)?

_____

_____

_____

HOPEFUL LEADERSHIP

Pray that the Spirit would help you hope in God's character.

Read Jonah 3:1–10. Reflect on Jonah 3:6–9.

Like the people of the city, the king of Nineveh repents and wears sackcloth in response to Jonah's message. He goes even further by sitting in ashes, another sign of mourning (see Esth 4:1; Jer 6:26; Dan 9:3). The king took action by issuing a proclamation for all of Nineveh to fast, mourn, repent and call on God. This is the second time in Jonah that non-Israelites have called on God (see Jonah 1:14).

Jonah's message did not seem to include an option for Nineveh's salvation. What does the king's willingness to humble himself and repent tell us about his character?

_____

_____

_____

_____

Notice the king's reasoning in 3:9. Do you think he was expecting God to relent? He was willing to humble himself and call out to God for deliverance— with only the hope that God might relent. How should this encourage those of us who know God's character (see 4:2) to humbly look to Him for help in times of trouble?

_____

_____

_____

_____

LESSON 5

GOD'S FORGIVENESS

Pray that the Lord would renew your appreciation of His grace and forgiveness.

Read Jonah 3:1–4:4. Reflect on Jonah 3:10.

Jonah 3:10 can be seen as the key verse of the book. After seeing the Ninevites' response, God had compassion on the city and decided not to destroy it. What does this show about God's desires for humanity?

_____

_____

_____

Notice the order of events in 3:10. God turned from the disaster only after the city repented. Read Exodus 32:9–14, 2 Samuel 24:11–17, Jeremiah 18:7–8 and Amos 7:1–6. What do these passages show us about repentance and God's judgment?

_____

_____

_____

_____

Describe what role repentance plays in your life. What steps can you take to ensure repentance is part of your daily life?

_____

_____

_____

_____

God's forgiveness of the Ninevites is not surprising to modern readers who know the story—or even to Jonah, who expected God to show mercy. But God's action would have surprised the original readers of the book. The Assyrians were known for their violence and cruelty. They proudly recorded their methods of torturing captives, and they displayed their victims' body parts throughout their cities. The level of their violence rivals that of Hitler or Pol Pot. To someone living in the ancient world, Nineveh would be least deserving of God's grace.

Considering the severity of Nineveh's evil, what does the extent of God's grace and forgiveness tell you about His character?

_____

_____

_____

Think of someone who is guilty of despicable acts today. How would you feel if they repented and God forgave them? Would you react with anger or praise, and why?

_____

_____

_____

AN ANGRY PRAYER

 Praise God for being gracious and compassionate, slow to anger and abounding in steadfast love.

Read Jonah 3:6–4:8. Reflect on Jonah 4:1–4.

Angered by God's forgiveness of Nineveh, Jonah prays for the second time in the book. Compare Jonah's first prayer in 2:1–9 with his prayer in 4:2–3. What changes between his first prayer and his second?

_____

_____

_____

What are Jonah's expectations for God's mercy? How does Jonah's attitude change when God's compassion is directed toward Nineveh rather than him?

_____

_____

_____

It's easy to think less of Jonah for his anger about Nineveh's salvation, but remember the severity of Nineveh's crimes. Jonah may have felt that, by not destroying the city, God was not bringing about justice. Think of a situation where someone did something deserving of punishment. How would you have felt if they were forgiven instead? Would it make a difference to you if they had repented? Would you have been able to forgive them?

_____

_____

_____

How does Jonah describe God? Read Exodus 34:6–7. What stands out to you about these descriptions?

_____

_____

_____

Jonah understood God's character, but he didn't share God's heart. Does your knowledge of God extend from your head to your heart?

_____

_____

_____

Read Ephesians 4:32–5:2. What does it mean to be an "imitator of God"?

_____

_____

_____

A PROPHET AND A PLANT

Pray that you would not take God's provision for granted.

Read Jonah 3:10–4:11. Reflect on Jonah 4:5–8.

Jonah did not answer God's question, "Is it right for you to be angry?" (4:4). Instead, he left Nineveh to see what would happen to the city. He may have been hoping that God would still destroy it. Compare Jonah's attitude toward Nineveh with Abraham's attitude toward Sodom in Genesis 18:22–33.

Throughout Jonah 4:5–8, God displays His ability to control nature. Just as He "appointed" a great fish in 1:17, God appoints a plant, a worm and a scorching wind. In doing so, He confirms Jonah's description of Him in 1:9. How did Jonah react to the plant? Compare that to his reaction to the scorching wind after the worm had destroyed the plant. Compare Job's response to his much greater loss in Job 1:21 and 2:10.

_____

_____

_____

_____

Think of times in your life when God has provided for you. How did you respond? Has God ever provided for you in a different way than you wanted or expected? How did you respond then?

_____

_____

_____

_____

MISPLACED PRIORITIES

 Pray that God would help your priorities to fall in line with Christ's priorities.

Read Jonah 4:1–11. Reflect on Jonah 4:9–11.

In this section, God points out the folly of Jonah's anger and asks him again whether his anger is appropriate. This time—frustrated that God has taken away his plant—Jonah answers that yes, his anger is indeed appropriate. God's response reveals just how misplaced Jonah's priorities are: Jonah cares more about a plant than an entire city.

What point do you think God is making by comparing Jonah's concern for the plant with His own concern for Nineveh? Is Jonah's concern for the plant altruistic or selfish?

_____

_____

_____

_____

_____

Make a list of the things you feel are important throughout your day. Do your daily concerns focus on the well-being of others or yourself? How many of your priorities would also be priorities for God?

_____

_____

_____

_____

_____

God makes it clear to Jonah that the "great city" of Nineveh is His priority. Read Deuteronomy 10:12, Micah 6:8, Matthew 6:26-33, Mark 12:28-34, 1 Timothy 2:1-4 and 2 Peter 3:9. What do these passages reveal about what matters to God?

_____

_____

_____

How can you make sure that you are seeking what is important to God?

_____

_____

_____

What role does prayer play in ensuring that your priorities fall in line with God's?

_____

_____

_____

CONCLUSION

Many prophets serve as models of God's righteousness, but Jonah can't be counted among them. He was self-centered, took God's provisions for granted and pouted when God didn't act the way he wanted. His priorities were centered on his own comfort and desires. Yet by revealing all his faults, Jonah points to the qualities that followers of God should exhibit instead—obedience, selflessness, thankfulness and compassion.

Jonah's mismatched priorities should inspire us to make sure that we have the same concerns as God, who "wants all people to be saved and to come to a knowledge of the truth" (1 Tim 2:4). May we marvel at God's forgiveness and mercy and celebrate with Him when our enemies come to know Him.